A YEAR AROUND OUR HOUSE

IN WORDS AND WATERCOLOURS

BY KATE MEARS

Kate Mears

Kate Mears trained at Brighton Art College and worked for several years illustrating children's books. Since moving to Somerset more than twenty years ago she has divided her time between looking after her family, painting, illustrating and gardening.
www.katemears.com

First published in 2011 by Kate Mears

ISBN 978-0-9569926-0-4

Edited by Mary Maher

Designed by Simon Mears

Printed in England by Four Way Print Limited

The Vicarage 'is beautifully situated in a well-wooded park, and from the back is an extensive view over the moor and a large expanse of country beyond. The vicar of North Curry has every reason to be proud of his splendid church and beautifully situated vicarage, and may justly consider that his lines have fallen in pleasant places.'

NORTH CURRY: ANCIENT MANOR AND HUNDRED
By Hugh Olivey
Barnicott & Pearce, Athenaeum Press 1901

December 1994

Foreword

The house we moved into in 1994 appeared to be a typical former Georgian vicarage, if rather shabby and worn at the edges. An underground passageway with an early stone-carved window, glitzy door handles throughout the house and the twinkles in the eyes of some of the older male villagers when I said where we lived, suggested otherwise.

I live in North Curry, a village in Somerset, with my husband Simon and our four children. In the sixteen years we've lived here I have gathered bits and pieces of information about the history of the house as they've arisen and kept them in vague chronological order in an untidy and ever expanding folder next to files of household bills and bank statements in what we call The Dog Food Cupboard in the kitchen.

In between times family life buzzed along while I painted and illustrated, using the house, garden and village as my main inspirations. The idea of linking my paintings with my increasing interest in the history of the house came when I wanted a coherent theme for an exhibition. The exhibition was booked for a year in advance. And so I made a note of most days' happenings in a diary from the first day of January, painting as I went along. I sought out more information from local records but mostly from talking to people who have had connections with the house. It's the memories of the living, hearsay, and remembered snippets that, for me, bring the house, our home, to life.

Assembling the journal became part of my day, a natural process, constantly adding and enriching it with newly gleaned information until, 'A Year Around our Our House' was born. It is an illustrated record of the passing seasons and the daily happenings in our home and in our village, while at the same time often reflecting on the foundations of our present life, the history of the place and some of its past inhabitants.

HOUSE HISTORY

Our village stands on a ridge above the Somerset levels and moors which are barely seven metres above sea level. The parish was once a Saxon Royal Manor, which passed to William at The Conquest. In 1189, Richard 1 sold the manor to the Dean and Chapter of Wells. The Dean and Chapter were lords of the manor for almost 700 years until 1866, when all Church of England estates were handed over to the Ecclesiastical Commissioners from which date, tenants were able to buy their properties. This house, however, remained the property of the church until 1938 when it ceased to be a vicarage.

15th century
The window in the cellar, a churchy affair, is the clue to the age of an earlier dwelling on top of which the present house was built. The window is partly obscured by a 19th century pillar supporting brick vaulting. From an informal chat with someone who knows about these things, I learned that the depth of carving is indicative of the 1400s, pre-Reformation.

I was told the window would have been shuttered and never glazed and that it is not a pirate piece, meaning it was built in situe and not pinched from some local ruin. Stonemason friends have told me that the large Hamstone blocks of the outer walls of the cellar would have been very expensive, which suggests this was a building of some importance, perhaps connected with the church. Rumour has it that monks lived here and that the silted-up pond north of the house known as The Monks' Pond is where they kept their fish. Monks Walk runs from the road at the end of our drive towards the centre of the village. The Abbey of Athelney, founded by King Alfred c.888 and surrendered in 1537 at the Dissolution of the Monasteries, held nine acres in the parish wherein may lie the connection, but I have as yet found no proof of this.

The window looks out onto an underground passageway running around the house, which must once have been open to the sky. Lesser Horseshoe bats roost in the cellar, flying in and out through the window.

The Monks' Pond

1714

The earliest written record of a dwelling on this site is in a Court Roll, a record of rent paid and property held by tenants, in this instance, Elizabeth Brewer in the west part of the house and James Dibben with his sisters Sarah and Mary in the east part. There is mention of kitchen and beer cellar, carthouse and wellhouse, pig sty and ox stall, orchards and ditches.

1787

A survey with accompanying map of the Manors of North Curry and neighbouring villages lists the tenants at Parsonage House as John and Stacey Seymour.

1815

This house was built by Charles Holcombe Dare on the remains of an earlier dwelling. Charles Dare, born in 1784 in the neighbouring village of Stoke St. Gregory, was a landowner, farmer and later a Lay Rector. He married Mary Frances Young Coker, sister of William King Coker, Vicar of North Curry 1820-1845. I can imagine their introduction, the consideration of the suitability of the match, or perhaps love at first sight, the ensuing courtship over tea at the Vicarage in Church Road and strolls in the shrubbery.

Some forty years later in the 1861 census, Charles and Mary are listed as aged 75 and 60 respectively, he an Impropriator Rector, living in this house, which was The Parsonage, with four live-in servants: Ann Lockyer aged 40, cook, Susanna Payne, 26, house servant, Eliza Durham, 14, house servant, and Sarah Hector, a 48 year old widow, nurse.

1820

Charles William Dare was born, eldest of Charles and Mary's three sons and a daughter. This house passed to Charles William on his father's death. Charles William Dare became a barrister and lived in Fosse Cottage at the end of the drive. He is buried in the churchyard, the back of this house just visible from his memorial.

His son, Edmund Coker Dare, was a planter in India. When he contracted malaria he returned to live with his parents in North Curry and was very involved in the life of the village as a Parish Councillor and on various village committees.

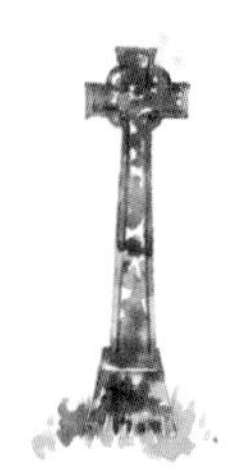

The Old Vicarage

1867

The Reverend Christopher Robert Harrison became Vicar of North Curry. The west window in the church is in his memory and contains his portrait and also that of his son who fell at Majuba Hill in 1881 in The First Boer War.

1871

The inhabitants of Parsonage House are listed in the 1871 census as George W. Mitchell, 46, from Chard, retired wine merchant, and his wife Sofia, 42, from Taunton. Also resident were Ann Venn, 55, an aunt from Pitminster, and two servants: cook Emma Smith, 28, born in North Curry, and housemaid Leanorah Champ, 18, from Lyme Regis. This must have been towards the end of their tenancy since, in the same year, The Vicarage was relocated to Parsonage House which was renamed The Vicarage.

1875

Extensive building works were undertaken at the new vicarage with alterations and a service wing added at a cost of £690. The old offices of kitchen, scullery, dairy and pantry behind the house were pulled down and rebuilt to the side. The mortgage application documents held in the Somerset Records Office have a detailed description of the existing house and the works to be carried out, down to the new lavatory seats, Honduras Mahogany, and for the servants, Deal.

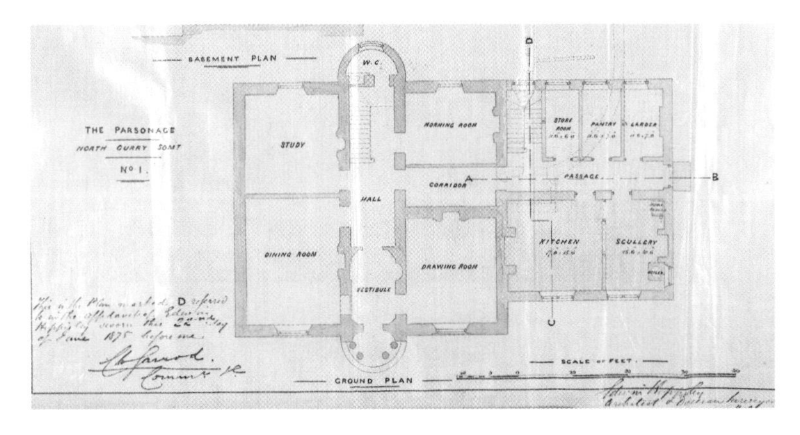

Ground floor plans 1875

1877

Vicar: Reverend Robert Charles Lathom Browne. The 1881 census lists the inhabitants of The Vicarage as Robert C.L. Browne, 36, born in Paddington, his wife Florence, 26, from Devon, and three live-in servants: 37 year old housemaid Harriett Tucker, a widow from Somerset, cook Alice Jane Short, 24, from Dorset, and groom George B. Tucker, 15, born in North Curry, presumably Harriett's son.

1890

Vicar: Reverend William Edmund Buller, who conducted the funeral of Charles William Dare on 14th October 1898. The 1891 census shows that the unmarried Reverend Buller was at this time 59, and shared his vicarage with his two unmarried sisters, Ann, 57, and Marian, 56, both listed as living on their own means. There were two live-in servants: Susan Liddon, 24, cook, and Emma Stephens, 26, housemaid, both unmarried and both local women born in North Curry.

1901

Vicar: Reverend Daniel James Pring. The 1901 census lists the inhabitants of The Vicarage as Reverend Pring, 41, his wife Emilie, 41, daughter Dorothea, 13, son Christopher, 1, and three servants: Sarah the cook aged 25, Alice the housemaid, 15, and Annie, 26, the nurse. The head gardener was a fellow called Tucker.

The Parish Magazine, started by Reverend Pring in 1903, has several references to The Vicarage and its role in the community throughout his incumbency of more than a quarter of a century.

The Vicarage c.1910 with bay windows, a conservatory and The West Door.

1918

One H. Denman picked over the potatoes, and in pencil recorded his task and signed his name on Feb. 4th 1918 on the central pillar in the far cellar room. I went to see Betty in the Village Archives to find out more. Harry Denman was known to everyone as Bob. He was 17 at the time, born 1901, the middle of five children. He lived with his family in The School House, just across the churchyard. His father Sydney was a chauffeur but died aged 50 later that year in August 1918. His mother Ann helped with cleaning and school meals at the school for years and died in 1963 aged 92. Bob's eldest sister Beatrice was married to Fred Lock, landlord of The White Hart and later Head Gardener at The Vicarage.

Nine years later another added his mark to the same pillar: G. Wembridge, Knapp.

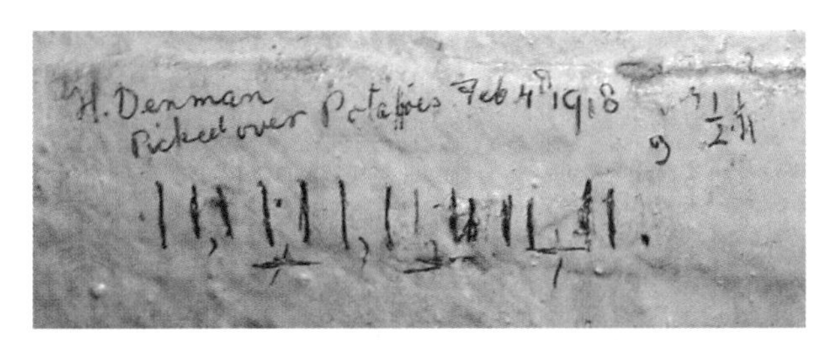

1928 Reverend Albion Kirk.
He was the last vicar to keep a horse in the Stables.

1931

Vicar: Reverend Augustus Gossage-Robinson. Reverend Robinson had the house wired for electricity with a generator installed in the stables. He put in new arch-topped windows on the first floor at the front. The Cornish plasterwork of the arches required a specialist plasterer to travel up from Cornwall to do the work. Mrs Robinson grew hyacinths in the wine cellar. Head gardener was Fred Lock who was also landlord of The White Hart Public House in Knapp Lane (his wife Beatrice ran the pub during the day).

The Vicarage c. 1932

Reverend Gossage-Robinson, back row left. Middle row 2nd to right is 'Young Webb' of the Boxing Tournament that appears later.

Vicarage staff 1930s during Reverend Robinson's incumbency.

Back row: Fred Lock, head gardener, Mabel Harris, parlour maid . Front row left to right: Minnie Hector, tweenie, Charlie Verrier, garden boy, Evelyn Bond, cook. Charlie, who lent me the photo, said a sixth member of staff took the picture.

1936

Vicar: Reverend Jocelyn Davies under whose incumbency The Vicarage was relocated to Moor Lane. Reverend Davies, a big man and former heavy weight boxer, was an ex naval man with no private income (one indication of which being that his daughters had to go out to work) and not all the staff were retained. The gardens fell into neglect. Charlie Verrier went to work in Stoke St Gregory.

1938

The last funfair and steamfair (Tamsin's of Weymouth) was held in The Vicarage grounds.

1938

The newly named Manor House was bought by Mrs Ella Frances Stobart, a wealthy widow. Mrs Stobart embarked straight away on major alterations, modernisations and building works which included rewiring, connecting the house to the national grid and the installation of central heating. Her building contractor was Gardiner's of Bristol, although Mrs Stobart chose to use mostly local men for the work.

The Manor house 1938

Mrs Stobart

The end result was a smart art deco villa most unlike the original Regency Parsonage. The substantial works to house and garden cost Mrs Stobart more than she paid for the whole place with its twenty two acres.

1945

Mrs Stobart asked Charlie Verrier, who had been home from the war a mere fortnight, to take up his old job as gardener at The Manor House. Mrs Stobart lived here until her death in 1955. Her memorial is set into the churchyard wall next to the gate which once led to The Manor House by way of a shortcut under the trees, across a wooden bridge, through an iron gate and up a few steps.

1955

Mrs Fox (Florence Mabel Hollams R.A. renowned painter of horses and dogs), an elderly widow, moved here from Kent to be near her son and family at Thornfalcon, a neighbouring hamlet. Mrs Fox had a Bentley driven by Bulworthy the chauffeur who lived in Manor Bungalow, which Mrs Fox had built for him. Mr and Mrs Creek, her butler and cook, came with her from Kent and lived in the servants' quarters behind the green baize door. The gardener lived in Manor Lodge. Her studio was in what is now our bathroom. She had a grand piano in the drawing room and took tea in the summer house (in Manor End's garden). She had enormous bonfires at the turn of the front drive, which did not impress former garden staff whose impeccably high standards had extended to picking every dead fallen leaf out of shrubs by hand.

Mrs Fox died here in March 1963.

The Manor House 1960s, the productive vegetable garden of less than a decade earlier, overgrown and untended.

1964

The Manor House was bought by Brian and Jennifer Webb and opened as The Glendorgal Country Club. We've had some visitors who'd not been here since the club days: a builder recalled the one-armed bandit slot machines in the ballroom (our drawing room); a mechanic returning our car was very excited to point out where he'd stood on stage as a nineteen year old drummer in a band. The ballroom had a sprung floor and stars painted on the ceiling. The bar was in our sitting room and the Tangier Restaurant was in Manor End. Wedding receptions were held here. I've had mention of 'ladies' from London, Bristol or Birmingham, depending on who I was talking to, although, "Yes, there were a bit o' tha'," is the nearest I've come to any elaboration on that subject. Word has recently reached me via Hong Kong through a family connection in the village, of a stripper at a barristers' convention. The vicars must be turning in their graves.

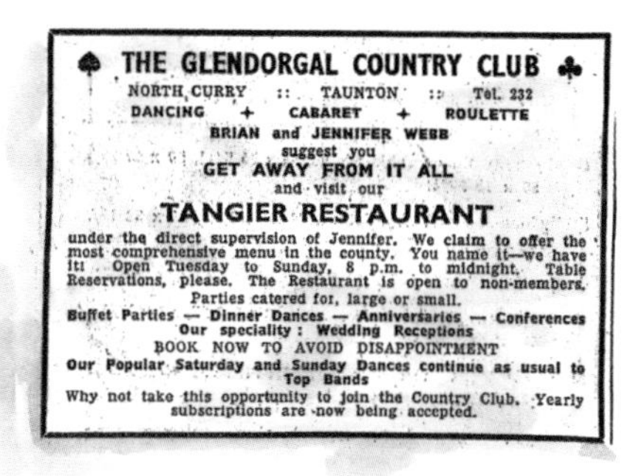

1968

The sale and division of The Manor House and surrounding fields and buildings took place. The sale, which was spread over two days, was poorly attended due to expectations of a high price when in fact the Lots went for surprisingly little.

1969

The Manor House reverted to a private residence and was divided into two houses, the service wing becoming Manor End.

1969-1994

Four sets of owners of The Manor House: a couple, two families and another couple and their two granddaughters. One of the fathers had plans to run a model railway up and down the drive, but ran off instead with his secretary. The other father cut short his family's time here by a dalliance with the au pair. One fellow was an engineer and a sculptor; his studio was still dusty with clay when we came here.

1994

We moved in.

January

1st Jan.
Roast goose & apple sauce for lunch this New Year's Day, reared in an orchard down the road. Christmas decorations will linger for a few days yet. The front door wreath is the centrepiece of the Christmas card I painted with a light dusting of snow.

3rd Jan.
A glorious sunny day. Simon & I walked the dogs around the field & through the churchyard. The slanting late afternoon sunshine was turning the church a golden hue.

January

Calmady House

I've had my eye on this view for a painting for some time. I sat on a gravestone to capture this one cold day when the light was as I liked it. I hadn't realised what a busy place the churchyard is - walkers, visitors to the church, the postman on his rounds. The cat from Gwyon House kept me company for a while.

10th Jan.

From 'Nature Notes', a parishioner's regular contribution to the monthly church magazine: 'The very cold weather lasting from late 4th December until the 10th January brought the most beautiful scenes of hoar frost..... For a hoar frost to form the night has to be clear & calm & the temperature of the surfaces of the plants has to become lower than freezing point causing the dew falling on them to freeze.'

January

The drawing room was originally two rooms, this end being the Victorian study where perhaps Reverend Pring wrote his Parish Magazine, and where Reverend Robinson would receive his parishioners.

By the 1930s The West Door had been installed, opening onto a newly constructed corridor. Parishioners would call at this door & get a glimpse, if all the doors were open, of a view right through the house from west to east out to the garden beyond (now Manor End's).

The sun still streams in here but through a window, & rests on the old green baize door in the hall now our coat cupboard, beyond which the view once stretched.

January

This end of the drawing room was the Victorian dining room &, ninety or so years later, bands performed on stage here for The Glendorgal Country Club.

This room is so
beautiful when
it is flooded
with sunlight,
which is why
I keep painting it.
It is also the only
time it is warm.

Fireplace, drawing room

January

12th Jan.
From the kitchen window I watched long-tailed tits at the feeder in the laburnum tree at the back. A vixen was calling all through the night, very close. The dogs chased her off across the field when I let them out this morning.

14th Jan.
The 1911 Census became available online this week. Curious to learn more of previous inhabitants of this house, I looked it up to find: Gerard M. Mason, 54, & his Spanish born wife Cristina, 52. They had no children. Two servants lived in: Lilian Stone, 25, housemaid, & Mabel Scriven, 25, cook. Further research revealed that Reverend Mason was vicar here for just 6 months whilst the incumbent, Reverend Pring, took an enforced 6 month holiday due to ill health.
I spend the day imagining the comings & goings in this house of these people whose names I have just learned.

15th Jan.
I sat & painted the dresser at the kitchen table in what was the morningroom in the house's vicarage days, & cook's bedroom in Reverend Robinson's time. Cook sometimes found it difficult to get to sleep when evening visitors of Reverend Robinson's son & daughter took their time to leave & stood chatting in the hall on the other side of the green baize door (which now opens onto the coat cupboard in the hall). In Mrs Stobart's time this room served as a formal receiving room & is where she & Charlie Verrier sat at a table to discuss his return to her employ in 1945 when he returned from the war.

JAMES
KATE

January

17th Jan.
Gale force winds & rain. Walking round to supper at John & Margaret's, we passed a large trampoline blown out onto Stoke Road. A few hours later on our way home the storm had blown over & all was still & quiet, apart from tawny owls & a disturbed rook or two in the trees along our drive.

Land girls Lily Haycourt & Cathy Otter, left & second left, who were billeted with Mr & Mrs Edwards in Stoke Road during the war. The Land Army Depot was just along the road at The Warren.

John & Margaret's house was built by Mrs Stobart in 1939 for her chauffeur Arthur Edwards, his wife & three children, Charlie, Sydney & June. I have learned more from Charlie Verrier, gardener here at The Manor House, who knew the family. Mrs Stobart's Rolls Royce had been a gift to her from her late husband, Major Stobart. It was Edwards' job to drive the chassis from the factory to the coachbuilders to have the body fitted. An orange box was the usual makeshift driver's seat for this, the car's first journey. The car was kept in the garage, the former stables, where heating was installed. Edwards drove the warmed car every Wednesday morning round to the front of The Manor House from where, at 9 o'clock, Mrs Stobart set off for her weekly shopping trip. She once asked Edwards how many miles to the gallon the car did & was told that it wasn't so much miles to the gallon as 'gallons to the mile, ma'am.'

January

Petrol rationing in World War II meant only enough fuel for one shopping trip a month, so the Rolls Royce went to Marshalls Garage in Taunton, & with it, Edwards the chauffeur. Given menial tasks at the garage, Edwards was not happy at work. At home the family had two land girls billeted with them. Arthur's eldest son, a pilot in the R.A.F., was killed in the war. His name is on the War Memorial in Queen Square.
Arthur Edwards died in 1946.

January

Stoke Road has housed a tannery, basket maker, stables, abattoir, bank, dressmakers, tailors, saddlers, wool shop, iron mongers & an inn, The Angel.
Betty, whose family have lived in the same house in Stoke Road since 1947, remembers her father chuckling over an exchange in The Angel in the late 1950s: a colonel living nearby was heard to address the butler of The Manor House by his surname, Creek. "I'm not your bloody Batman" was the indignant response.

Up until halfway through the twentieth century, Stoke Road was named as such only as far as the White Street turning, beyond which it was Pury Street, leading to Pury Farm on the outskirts of the village towards Stoke St. Gregory. In the official naming of roads, other names have been lost or moved, for example, The Pavement in the centre of the village used to refer to the stretch of slippery path along Church Road.

January

18th Jan.
The aconites are out along the drive, there are primroses in the old Ha Ha bed, & snowdrops appearing around the urn under the trees (the burial place of guinea pigs, hamsters, gerbils & budgies).

I cycled up with oboe & music stand in my bicycle basket to orchestra practice in the village hall this morning. The first North Curry Orchestra concert I took part in two or three years ago had the unusual programme combination of The Sound of Music (sing along) & Haydn.

This little jug is a stray from a set of china from which my great great grandparents (born 1830s) drank tea at their farm in Kent, and mentioned in a book about his childhood, 'The Small Years' by Frank Kendon, my great uncle.

January

26th Jan.

First eggs of the year AT LAST. Our bantams may be pretty but they are very fickle about egg laying. We have two cockerels who get along fine, & a selection of hens.

31st Jan.

Our chocolate Labrador Bruno has been up to his old tricks & sneaked off for a sniff-about. He's very crafty in that for weeks he shows no interest in straying & our guard is dropped, & then he will just disappear. Apart from the worry of the danger to him & others on the roads, it is intensely irritating & time consuming during the ensuing search, which is usually fruitless as I am convinced he hears us & hides. People are very kind in returning him to us or giving us a ring as to his whereabouts. This time he was at the shop behind the counter with Alison & Janet by the time Chris & James arrived to bring him home.

February

2nd Feb.
SNOW! Fat, flurrying flakes. The boys, home from school & college, set off at dusk with the dogs to toboggan on the north slope behind the house.
I walked up to a 7.30pm meeting in The Coffee Shop. On my way home in the quiet of snowfall, with no cars, my route was lit by people's front door lights; no street lights in the centre of the village. My footsteps were the first prints in two inches of fresh snow.

6th Feb.
Snowed in. We're unable to get to work, school or college. The roads are like an ice rink since there's been no gritting in the village. I sense a festival atmosphere with what seems like most of the village gravitating towards the toboggan slope behind the house.

8th Feb.
The line-up along our drive this morning consisted of our car, the doctor's landrover, a fire crew landrover, an ambulance & finally, a tractor called up to pull out the stuck ambulance which had been summoned to rescue an injured tobogganer from the field.

We have had our second visit of fox or badger by day - four bantams are gone.

February

11th Feb.
Today there is thick fog, & floods everywhere
from melting snow & heavy rain yesterday.
The moor road is impassable. Stoke Road
is flooded from the end of the Moredon
Drive right up to Pury Farm. Ham village
is flooded. The only way out of the
village is via Thornfalcon & long traffic
queues.

12th Feb.
This morning was bright & cold with mist over the moor.
I heard my first woodpecker of the year drilling away
at the tall oak along The Fosse.

24th Feb.
Our neighbour John brought
round the bowl he's turned
from a piece of one of the balsam
poplars planted by Mrs Fox in
the early 1960s along the field
fence. They were becoming
diseased & dangerous & we had
them felled a couple of years
ago, replanting with five oaks,
Quercus robur fastigiata.

I have been given rolls of old ordnance survey maps from an attic clearout.
I have cut out the North Curry section & painted in, with reference to the Environment Agency flood map, the areas which often flood in winter, almost cutting off the village.
King Alfred's base at Athelney is a little island in a marshy sea.

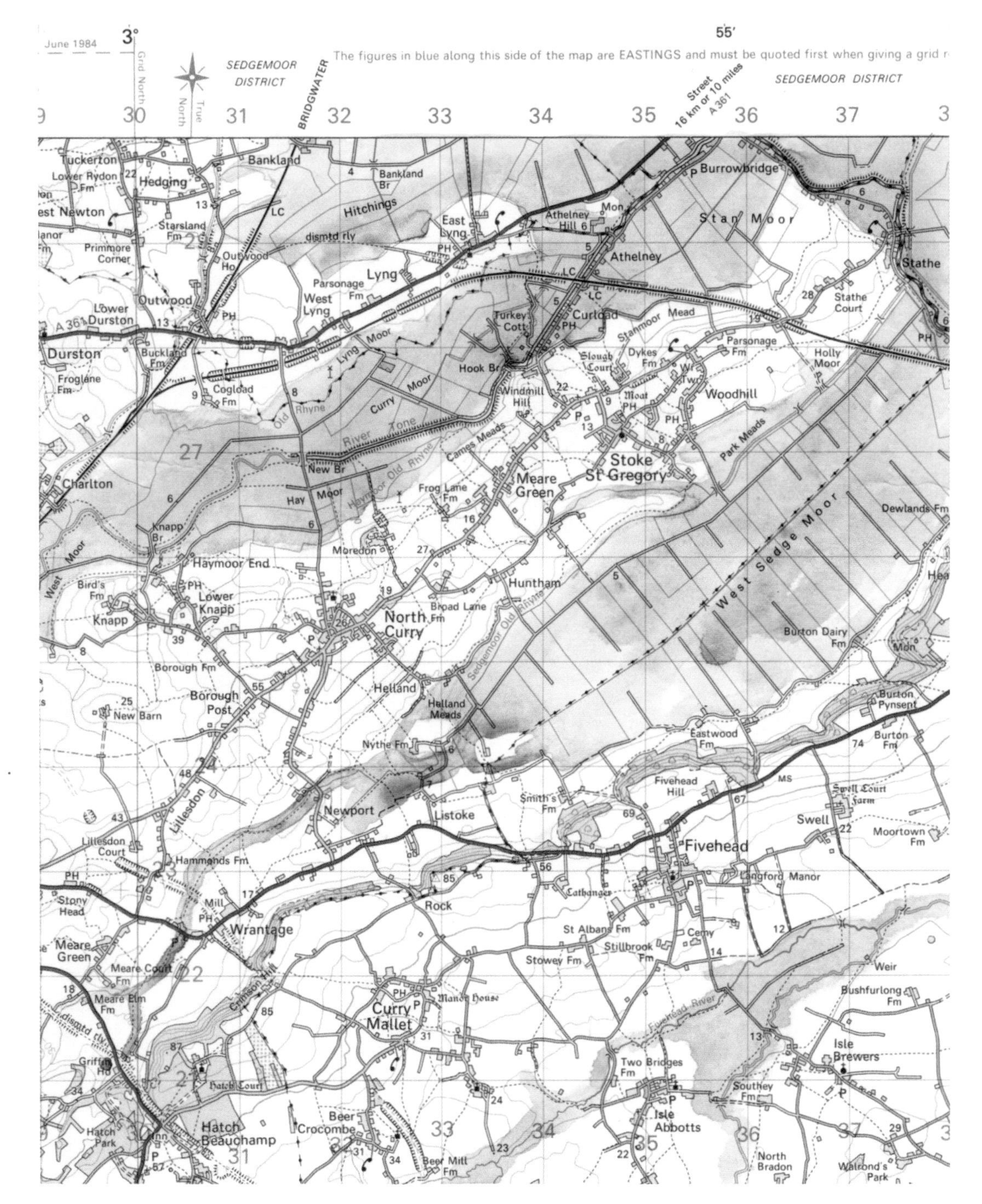

March

2nd March
Marian called in for a cup of tea on her way home with a dead pheasant in her car boot, road kill, still warm. She'd phoned her man Bill to say supper was sorted & he said he had a deer in <u>his</u> boot; slight twinge of inadequacy in relation to these friends who are not too squeamish to transform feathers & fur into a good meal when the opportunity presents itself.

3rd March
Over coffee at Mary's house in Queen Square I learned more about her grandmother Mrs Fox who lived in our house from 1957-1963. Mrs Fox went to her granddaughter's wedding in London in January 1962 & was driven there & back in the Bentley on the day by Bulworthy the chauffeur.

7th March
Mike Hutchings, delivering kindling at the front door, said they'd come to the Glendorgal Club after the pubs closed. He told me many a night's been spent here that wasn't remembered. Mike, before he retired, ran Hutchings shop in Queen Square with his brother Ken & their father before them.

London House, Queen Square, formerly London House Stores

9th March
Sunny, blustery day. The first anenomes are open along the drive - brought back from Switzerland in the 1870s by Reverend Harrison as rumour has it. He was the first vicar to live in this house when it became the Vicarage. Anenomes also carpet the churchyard.

Fosse Cottage from the churchyard. Stand & study the walls of Fosse Cottage & you'll see the tops of recycled headstones in the stonework.

March

Our walk up to the village is along Church Road past dwellings that once housed....

a boot & shoe repairer.....

an ironmongers & a tailor's shop.

a saddlers, a coach house, a carpenter's shop....

On the west side of Queen Square; a drapers, a grocers, a hair dressers, an estate agents + a bakers.

In Queen Square; a baker, Hutchings' shop where you could buy almost anything, + the medieval village lock-up.

Jesters, the end of terrace cottage on Queen Square's west side, was reputed to have a ghost. I asked the people who were living there about their ghost. They said that, regular as clockwork at 9.20pm every evening, their windows rattled. In which case we too had a ghost since our windows did the same - it was the sonic boom of Concorde, which ceased in 2003 after Concorde's last flight.

March

18th March
I walked the dogs through the churchyard, up to Moredon & along the ridge past Frog Lane Farm. The heavy mist over the moor had almost dispersed & the recently spread muck was steaming all over the field below in the cold morning air.

View from Moredon

Frog Lane Farm

30th March
The two little black bantams are insistent on being broody dammit. I want eggs, not chicks. I have given in & begged some eggs from a friend because the silly things are sitting tight on nothing but straw. Three weeks from now, maybe we'll have some chicks?

April

12th April
Tulips are out everywhere - in the Ha Ha bed, the box bed at the side of the house, & in the pots around the back.

20th April
CHICKS! Three weeks to the day after I put eggs under our broody bantams, I peered into the nest box & a little yellow chick stared back. It always amazes me. By the end of the day we had six chicks. The image of that first peep is still with me like a little jewel imprinted on my memory together with the warm anticipation of showing James when he arrived home from school.

26th April
The fields around the house are a sea of buttercups.

27th April
At one o'clock on the way back from our Pink Sheet (monthly village newsletter) delivery round, I glanced into the back garden to see a fox ON the chicken run. I thought all the lifeless chicks scattered about the run were dead from shock, but placing them under a hen in the nest box revived them within an hour.

May

5th May
The irises are coming into flower under both windows at the front of the house; white, mauve, & two yellow which I moved from round the back a couple of years ago.

7th May
The horse chestnut in Manor Field is MAGNIFICENT
in its candled glory.

May

8th May
We joined friends for a Friday evening drink in the Bird in Hand, which has been selling beer since 1790. The bus stop for Taunton is on the pavement in front of the crooked sign. There are six buses a day, one about every two hours.

11th May
Chris passed his driving test today. I booked our summer hols - two weeks in Greece.

16th May
The annual May Fair in Church Road today. The showers held off.

'Edgeways' to the left in this terrace next to the pub
has been a butchers, a drapers, a boot makers &
then a butchers again until shortly before we
moved here in 1994 when there were five shops
in the village. Now there is just the Post Office/Stores.

May bluebells

May

30th May
Roses, roses all around the house. Over the willow arch in the back garden Madame Alfred Carrière gives us two flowerings each summer. The back garden had descended into a wilderness when Mrs Stobart bought the house in 1938. I have learned from her gardener Charlie Verrier that she had it cleared & planted with daffodils + apple trees (Red Delicious inspired by a box of the same, sent as a Christmas present from her sister in Canada).

The nine-foot wide herbaceous border was created for Mrs Stobart in the late 1930s + ran the length of the vegetable garden wall. It has long since been grassed over, but the very productive fig tree next to the peony is a survivor from the 30s.

Beyond the back garden gate along the ridge overlooking the moor stood a number of elm trees known collectively as 'Rookery', obscuring the view we have today of the moor. The trees were cut down in the 1940s.

Mrs Stobart's back garden

June

4th June
In this glorious weather we have breakfast, lunch & supper outside.
The children have taken to walking the dogs after supper in the balmy midsummer dusk.

6th June
Simon & I drove to Langport this morning. I really like Langport. Its been said to be up & coming for the past 25 years, but its great as it is, especially for a caffeine fix from the proper espresso coffee in the café near the corner.

15th June

I dropped in for a cup of tea at Tamsin's in Stoke Road where she & her family have lived for six years; before them, the Goulds for twenty five years & before them, the Matthews for twenty five years. Mr Matthews was digging in the front garden when he came across, buried, the sawn-off barrel of an expensive shotgun with some bullets, all wrapped up in hessian. They still have the rusty piece stuffed in a cobwebby corner somewhere.

Thunder has been rolling around the house all afternoon making the windows rattle. I came across an old postcard in North Curry Archives of eight dead cows killed by lightening. It was at Hammonds Farm, Lillesdon, just up the road c. 1905. The farmer was Ernest Prew. I see his daughter around the village; she doesn't know me.

June

Our bedroom was the vicarage's master bedroom. Mrs Stobart had this room knocked through to the adjacent oriel window bedroom to form one large upstairs drawing room. The flower arrangements here & elsewhere in the house were attended to every morning by the outside staff who were allowed indoors for this task only. Carnations were available all year round from the Carnation House which Mrs Stobart had had built next to the large greenhouse in the vegetable garden. There were two flower arrangements on stands either side of the arch in the hall, another at the turn of the stairs. The lead-lined basket on legs in the big drawing room took 30 plants. The upstairs drawing room had a smaller version.

19th June
I awoke to see the cows very close, lying in the field just beyond the garden gate. While the kettle boiled for tea I stepped barefoot outside to smell the air & take in the breathy cows, cackling jackdaws, a heavy dew, the scent of honeysuckle & sunshine that sparkled.

The Manor House greenhouses in the walled vegetable garden.

Bruno surveying his domain from the front door & pretending he's not thinking about running off.

23rd June

This evening we frightened off a badger lurking near the chicken house. Poor Michèle opposite has lost a hen & chicks in their 'nursery', the greenhouse; a badger dug itself in overnight & ate the lot.

June

The Washroom

I used to think this room, downstairs on the ground floor at the back of the house was the Georgian kitchen, but 1875 documents show that the offices of kitchen, scullery, dairy & pantry were in a wing knocked down to make way for the building of the service wing that is now Manor End.

In the early 20th century Christopher Pring, son of Reverend Pring, used the room for his photography hobby. In the 1940s + 50s Mrs Stobart's staff stored their bicycles in here. But I can't help feeling that laundry, as today, has been done here before; in the soot-blackened brick + slate-lined recess where we store our logs, it has been suggested there would have hung a copper for boiling washing. Was the room conveniently warm from what I assume to be a bread oven, the large bricked-up bulge against which the boiler sits? I know that in the middle decades of the 20th century the household's washing was sent out: in the 1930s, Charlie the garden boy, would take the vicarage washing to Mrs Rowsell at number 6 Greenway. In the 40s + 50s, Mrs Stobart had a laundry van collect + deliver the laundry.

The washroom today has a Belfast sink & wooden drainer, two ceiling airers, the boiler, washing machine & plenty of storage space. It is where the dogs sleep at night & dry off after a muddy walk, and the subject of a piece of writing for which Lucy won a school prize when she was eight.

11-5-98

My Special place

My Special place is down in the wash room. because Dandelion, Inky, Chotate-drop, Hazel-nut and Chest-nut are down there. Chestnut and Hazel-nut are hamsters and the others are Gunipigs. When I go down there I get them out of their cages and play with them. They are all boys apart from Hazelnut. The gunipigs like eating vegeabols and grass and dandelions. The hamsters like eating carots. Dandelion, Inky, and chestnut are Eleanor's. Chotate-drop and hazelnut are my animus. I feel Happy and I have compony. I have compony because animals are arwnd me. I feel happy because I like playing with them.

July

1st July
Ponies on the loose, reported in this month's Pink Sheet. This is old news: it must be 2 years since I found myself driving up Greenway preceded by 3 galloping ponies, ropes & chains flying. They turned off into Portmans where I & a few others contained them for a while, watching them graze the lawns. The police turned up & the ponies galloped off. They come from the gypsy site at Oxen Lane, the subject of legal dispute since it was occupied 5 years ago.

12th July
Roast beef & Yorkshire puds for lunch, changeable weather. all very English for the visiting French boy. Gaétan, from Bordeaux.

16th July
We have had incessant rain these last ten days, & it is so cold I am wearing slippers.

Summer flowers in a painted pot that belonged to Margery, my maternal grandfather's cousin. I remember a painting on Margery's wall by her close friend Thomas Hennell, one of the artists commissioned for the 'Recording Britain' scheme set up in 1940 at the outbreak of the Second World War to make a visual record of British lives & landscapes at a time of imminent change. Thomas Hennell died in the Far East in November 1945, one of three war artists to die on active service.

July

July 1925
The Reverend Daniel Pring (vicar here 1901-28) writes in the Parish Magazine of phenomenally fine weather much appreciated by the hay makers after a damp previous two years (the hay makers this year are having a hard time of it). He records the Church Sale and Summer Fête held in the vicarage grounds, entrance by the vicarage front gate, the sale & side shows in the paddock, tea served on the lawn where a space was reserved for dancing. The gross takings were £182.5s.0d in aid of relighting the church.

The vicarage gates were sold for ten shillings by Mrs Stobart to be melted down for the war effort. A pre-war photo shows the old gates to be not dissimilar from the present ones.

17th July
Simon & I joined Eleanor at her graduation in Bath. We had lunch at the same restaurant in the city where we three ate when we took her up to Bath 3 years ago.

19th July
Today we leave for a night at Dave & Cathy's in Sussex before flying tomorrow to the heat & sun of Syros in the Greek Cyclades for a fortnight.

Eleanor's dressing table, her bedroom full of the afternoon sunshine.

August

4th August
After a sun-drenched two weeks we drove home from Gatwick in the pouring rain. It has rained every day we've been away.

6th August
Lucy & I had a 4am start, to take Lucy to Bristol airport. As I swung the car round, the headlights lit up a scene of devastation in the chicken run. Our fault - the one night we forgot to shut the run, something took the opportunity to have a feast, leaving nothing but feathers & a pair of perfect yellow feet standing as though the body had flown off without them. With a twinge of guilt I am feeling very sorry for the poor hens, but I can now go & get some Laying hens.

9th August
We continue to mow every week due to ideal growing conditions of frequent rain with sunny spells. The sense of gloom in those who've not escaped to some sunshine this summer is palpable.

10th August
James & I drove to Tiverton today to collect four fine Black Rock hens.

11th August
The figs in the back garden are ripening so quickly we are struggling to eat them all. The Discovery apples are falling & James is juicing them - their juice is sweet & pink.

August

12th August

We have embarked on a great reorganisation of the playroom into a studio for Simon & me. This room was originally the vicarage Parish Room, as mentioned by Reverend Pring in the Parish Magazine June 1909 on the carving & installation of a mantelshelf & two panels, sadly no longer there, either side of the fireplace.

The room also housed the Parish Lending Library, mentioned in the magazine's October 1919 issue as being reorganised & accommodated at the vicarage & numbering more than 1100 volumes.

In later years billiards was played here, the room serving as a kind of club. In the early 1930s, Reverend Robinson's time, chairs were stored here for events such as the Mothers' Union meetings held in the little room just inside the west door upstairs.

THE NORTH CURRY
PARISH
LENDING
LIBRARY

WILL RE-OPEN AT

The Vicarage "Parish Room,"

On Monday, Oct.

AT SIX P.M.

And each succeeding Monday during the Winter Months at the same hour.

TERMS OF SUBSCRIPTION.

Subscribers may have one volume per week throughout the season for every shilling subscribed.

E. GOODMAN AND SON, PHŒNIX PRINTING WORKS, NORTH STREET, TAUNTON.

15th August
I am harvesting my tomatoes (many rotten due to DAMP), beans, swiss chard, courgettes. The chickens adore bolted lettuces. Great eggs.

17th August
Someone told me today whilst we were chatting on the front doorstep, that he'd found a truffle a few years ago under the tall oak opposite along the Fosse. He grated it into an omelette.

22nd August
The cyclamen in flower beneath the big lime tree are a carpet of pink & white.

August

26th August
The Meteorological Office, explaining away its false promise of a barbecue summer, says the fault lies with the unpredictability of the jet stream which has been sitting further south than usual, causing these weeks & weeks of unsettled weather. Today, driving rain, grey, wet, green, dull.

September

2nd September
James is back at school today.

8th September
The glorious oak in the field east of the house (Home Field on old maps) has shed a huge branch. We have watched a number of trees in these fields deteriorate & disappear. The 'well-wooded park' of more than a hundred years ago is sadly depleted.

September

9th September

Four of us sat in Anna's garden drinking coffee & talking loudly over the perfect peals of a visiting band of bellringers. I used to bellring here & as a teenager, but my hands still go clammy at the recollection. I never mastered the ease & style of some of the old boys who looked as though they could smoke a cigarette with one hand whilst ringing the bell with the other.

12th September

The air is full of dreamy autumn sunshine, gentle breezes, warmth, butterflies & dragonflies. The summer is a cold grey memory. I picked apples from the back garden to paint; the last of the Discovery, the Spartan almost ripe, & the ripe Jupiter & Bramley. The Russet, mostly dead, overcome by mistletoe, is now smothered in climbing rose & jasmine.

September

13th September
I arrived back from orchestra practice to find David & son Miles assisted by Simon, Chris & James, felling a young horse chestnut tree which has Bleeding Canker. This new disease is spreading across the country. Young trees quickly succumb & in dispatching this one we hope to protect the other huge old horse chestnuts along the drive.

14th September
Sitting at the kitchen table, I've just had lunch & the church clock is striking two. I'm looking through the steam of the mug of tea in my hands at the tall yellow daisies bright in the sunshine against the dark of the open garage. The moor beyond is a series of green strips under a soft grey sky, blue overhead. I'm still in flipflops, but socks are beckoning - the air is cold.
Chris back at college today.

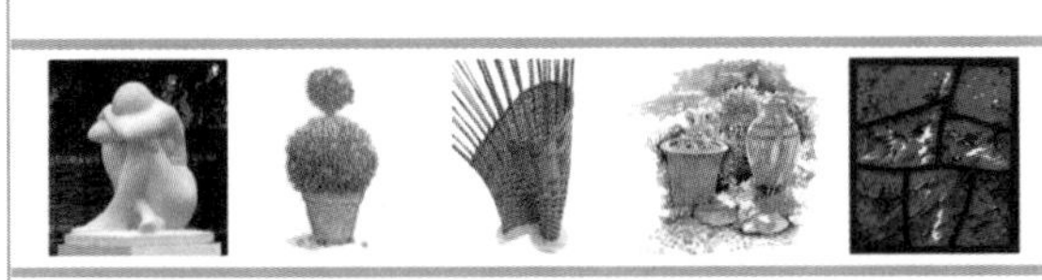

18th September
I spent the morning hanging my paintings in a shared exhibition for Somerset Art Weeks. There are five of us; sculpture, embroidery, willow, paintings, & stained glass.

A yell of 'CHICKENS' as one of us suddenly noticed the early unexpected dark of September evenings & we rushed to close up the run. I'm ashamed to think of how few of our hens have died of old age - our negligence, the fox & the badger have done for most of them.

September

22nd September
Walking the dogs, my eyes caught the scarlet of rosehips & the gleam of blackberries in the hedgerows. We are picking raspberries daily from along the fence outside the back door.

Some years ago a window cleaner, noticing a sick Light Sussex hen, offered to wring its neck. He did so whilst I walked up to school to collect James. We returned to a very edgy flock minus one.

Michele's Buff Sussex cockerel & our Light Sussex, who used to crow at each other across the Fosse.

30th September
Tamsin has rescued a lamb from the field behind her house, one of twins that appeared to be fading away. When she phoned the farmer he wasn't interested in saving the lamb. After a weekend of round the clock two hourly feeds, Orphan Annie is now with a friend who lives next to the churchyard where she takes Annie for walks.
A previous vicar kept goats in the graveyard; cheaper grass cutting than the annual £2000 it costs to keep the grass neat today.

October

3rd October
It was the monthly produce market in the Village Hall this morning. I bought some lamb from Lyng, a chocolate cake on a doily, a jar of jam + some lettuce + tomatoes from somebody's garden.

8th October
After yesterday's downpours, today was beautiful. I walked the dogs down over the moor & back up through Moredon, passing dewy cobwebs along my way & a late butterfly fluttering just above the lush grass. I felt the nip in the air, could see my breath, heard a buzzard calling, & a raven flew overhead rasping its deep croak.

October

The dogs move around the house with the sun. This is their morning spot, in the sitting room.

12th October
The carpenter repairing our windows grew up in North Curry & left when he married in 1976. Chatting, he recalled the self-sufficiency of the village with its range of shops & trades. He knew this house & remembered a metal arch strung with coloured lights at the entrance to the back drive which led to parking behind the house in its country club days. He & his mates, catapults then the school craze, would take pot shots at the light bulbs.

14th October
Simon said to Bob the carpenter this morning, "Lovely day." "Every day's a nice day if you're watching the grass grow on the right side," was the reply.

The little blue door at the back of the house opens onto an underground passageway. Charlie Verrier has told me this is where the Parish Ladder was kept when the house was a vicarage, for use by all in the parish. It took 6 men to lift it.
This area of garden behind the house, now mostly gravelled, was lawn until tarmac was laid for the club's parking. It has a busy atmosphere + would have witnessed the criss-crossing of staff + tradesmen going to the Back Door (now at Manor End) + visitors to the vicarage Parish Room + later the Library, accessed through the Cellar Door (our back door).

October

October Pink Sheet
The 17th century building, until recently the White Hart pub in Knapp Lane, is well & truly gone: demolished last year despite considerable local opposition, the second planning application to erect 8 properties on the site has been approved.

19th October
On the day that the nationwide vaccination starts, Chris has gone down with swine 'flu.

29th October
I went with friends to a talk at Brendon Books in Taunton by the journalist & one time MP Martin Bell on his new book about the current MPs' expenses scandal.

30th October
Simon's 50th birthday. With Chris recovering from 'flu & Simon fighting off a chest infection we celebrated with a meet up & meal out for all 6 of us in Bath.

November

Kate Mears 2009

Hutchings Newsagents:
I'm glad our children knew Hutchings, the sort of shop that was becoming rare in my childhood.
You'd make your way around a multitude of goods on the raised paved area outside: flowers, bedding plants, seed stands, kindling, compost, brooms, fishing nets, bird tables, bicycles, lawn mowers, coal.
The interior was dark & crammed full. The long glass-fronted counter was covered with the daily newspapers. On shelves, in drawers & cabinets, you could usually find what you were looking for: stationery, haberdashery, fireworks, Wellington boots, picture books, sweets, chocolate, milk, tea, coffee & biscuits.
Up a rickety ladder as though to a hayloft were the video rentals; orange fluorescent sheets of paper addressed those who'd 'borrowed' the covers of the x-rated films, to return them. "We know who you are," they announced.

November

Some Points on "How Boxing is Judged"

BOXING TOURNAMENT

AT

NORTH CURRY

ON

SAT DAY, NOV. 12th

at 8 p.m.

SCORING

8 Rounds Challenge Contest at Catchweights

TED SHERWOOD, of Newtown.

Official Welterweight champion of Hampshire and holder of two valuable belts which will be on show. Sherwood has won over 260 contests against some of the best men in the country, including Jack Powell, Arnold Kid Shepherd, Buster Osborne, Paddy Roche, Jack Lewis and recently drew with Stoker Perks and Jack Marino.

V

ALBERT DOWNTON, of Chelbrough.

Lightweight Champion of Somerset. Undefeated this year, has defeated recently Young Ayley, Young Butler, Patsy Lynch, Jim Leonard, Ron Sully, Eddie Middle, etc. Downton has challenged Sherwood as he is sure he can defeat him. Downton's terrific punching against Sherwood's experience should prove the fight of the season.

8 Rounds Welterweight Contest

HAROLD WHELLER, of Langport.

A greatly improved fighter, has K.O.d Jack Weeks, Male, Bill Peaty, Ted Haskett, etc.

V

HAL SANSOM, of rnemouth.

A very clever welterweight, has defeated others, Francis Webster, Jack Thompson, Young Hanham, Billy Jukes

6 Rounds Lightweight Contest

YOUNG WEBB, of North Curry.

V

CHARLIE CH EY, of Taunton.

Interval minutes.

6 Rounds Contest

NORMAN HEMBROW, Stoke St. Gregory

A boy who caused a sensation at Langport on October 15th, when he put up a terrific slam.

V

STAN TRIM, of Barrow Bridge.

A hard punching boy who has put up several good fights in the district.

6 Rounds Featherweight Contest

JOHNNY WARE, of Parkstone.

A smashing young southpaw who defeated Sid Griffiths of Taunton, and is in training with Ted Sherwood.

V

YOUNG DDICE, of Bridgwater.

A very game st others has defeated Tommy Cox, etc.

Smashing 8 Roun Fe weight Contest

DICK WHELLER, of Langport.

The 16 year old wonder b a the opinion of many expert judges of boxing including two former european pions, is a potential champion. Has K.O.d Stan Trim in 1 round, Tomm rounds, Sid Griffiths twice in 3 & 4 rounds and defeated on points Bob twice, Tiger Bood, Jimmy Albin, Hamp and Dorset Champ

LEN HEYWO Bridgwater.

Record not t and, has defeated rweights in West of England. Heywood has challenged Wheller throu anager, on winner take all basis, and has been excepted by Wheller. This d be one of the best contests seen in the district.

6th November
Whilst the windows are being repainted I am reminded of when we unblocked the two centre windows in the drawing room in 1997.
Our builders found rubbish discarded by their predecessors: a time sheet of Hayward & Wooster Ltd., Bath, cigarette boxes (Craven A, Star, Gold Flake), & a boxing tournament programme.
I took the programme to Ken & Mike's shop, Hutchings, where I learned that "YOUNG WEBB of North Curry" was their cousin.
Hutchings was a companionable & busy place. A few of Ken & Mike's mates were sometimes at the counter passing the time of day. I once went in & heard the words, "You going to give Kate a pinch?" They were taking snuff.
Sad day when it closed due to Ken & Mike's retirement.

9th November
We went to life drawing at Drayton this evening.
Where the road rises up through the trees towards
Fivehead I once drove over the words, written
professionally in white line lettering, "Rain may
wash away the words but never my love for you."
It had gone the next time I went that way.

10th November
It's been a dull damp day but pale watery
sunshine broke through not long before
sunset. From the kitchen window I
watched mist fill the moor like dry ice.
Early owls were calling before dark
as I closed the chicken run.

11th November
I went today to visit Charlie & Pearl
Verrier in Taunton. Over a cup of tea
they filled me in with all sorts of
details about the people & routines
central to the running of this house
since the time of oil lamps, horses
& servants.

November

Mrs Stobart's household from 1938 comprised 5 indoor staff: a succession of cooks, Lucy the housemaid, Edwards the chauffeur, and a parlour maid & tweeny (between maid) who shared a bedroom in what is now our bathroom.

Charlie Verrier (left) and Bob Garwell on the Back Drive

There were four outdoor staff to maintain the extensive gardens which included the walled Vegetable Garden, the formal Paved Garden with its new pond & summer house (now Manor Ends), the Water Garden (under the wooden bridge at The Coach House) & the Tennis Court, which was actually the lawn but retained its name from years back when Reverend Pring had it laid out for his son Christopher. The lawn is now field beyond our garden fence. The 3 drives were The Front Drive, The Short Drive linking to The Back Drive.

Cows on 'the Tennis Court'

The Paved Garden

The Water Garden

The Garage, on the Back Drive

November

One of Charlie's jobs was to look after the central heating once Mrs Stobart had decided it should go on. To light the boiler Charlie would use: one faggot of wood, one wheelbarrow full of logs & two wheelbarrows of coal. He lit the boiler on the first day at 7am & it took until 4 o'clock in the afternoon for all the radiators to warm through as he bled each in turn. The heating stayed on until Spring, kept at 65 degrees Fahrenheit as instructed by Mrs Stobart. One cold season Charlie shovelled 11 tons of coal into the boiler. The coal store is now next door's study.

I

er Georgy Harris & his wife kept the garden going,
with many of the herbaceous beds. Help came
men joined up. Charlie was in the army in
t for 6 years. After the war there were only
taff; Margaret the cook & Lucy Coram from
erton, 'general dogsbody'. Charlie returned
for Mrs Stobart within a fortnight of his
om abroad. I asked Charlie if the gardens
their former glory. He said it took them a
a lot of work, but they got there eventually.
nagine him being satisfied with anything less.

November

Mrs Stobart had thoroughly modernised The Manor & kept it in the highest order. Despite the reduced staff during & after the war, standards did not drop. She was a respected employer, kind & fair, although she expected her staff to know their place. One prospective employee's relaxed stance of leaning against the door frame during his interview caused him to be dismissed forthwith.

When Mrs Stobart died the house was sold. A separate sale of the house contents was displayed in marquees on the lawn & lasted for 2 days.

By direction of the Executors of the Late Mrs. E. F. Stobart

SOMERSET

North Curry Manor

Near Taunton

FOR SALE BY AUCTION 1955

by

JACKSON-STOPS & STAFF

in conjunction with

ARTHUR W. GLASS

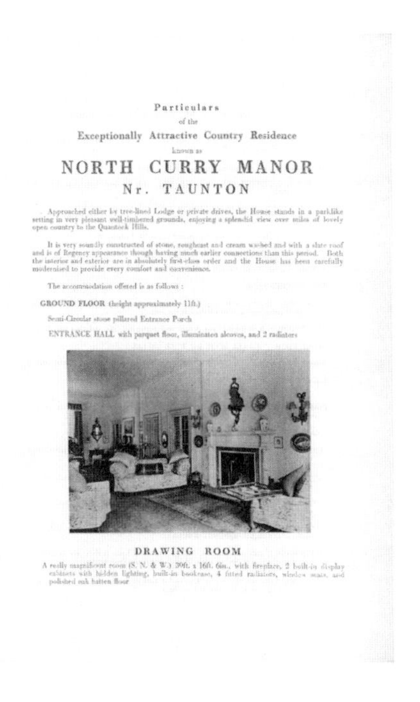

Particulars

of the

Exceptionally Attractive Country Residence

known as

NORTH CURRY MANOR

Nr. TAUNTON

Approached either by tree-lined Lodge or private drives, the House stands in a parklike setting in very pleasant well-timbered grounds, enjoying a splendid view over miles of lovely open country to the Quantock Hills.

It is very soundly constructed of stone, roughcast and cream washed and with a slate roof and is of Regency appearance though having much earlier connections than this period. Both the interior and exterior are in absolutely first-class order and the House has been carefully modernised to provide every comfort and convenience.

The accommodation offered is as follows :

GROUND FLOOR (height approximately 11ft.)

Semi-Circular stone pillared Entrance Porch

ENTRANCE HALL with parquet floor, illuminated alcoves, and 2 radiators

DRAWING ROOM

A really magnificent room (S. N. & W.) 39ft. x 16ft. 6in., with fireplace, 2 built-in display cabinets with hidden lighting, built-in bookcase, 4 fitted radiators, window seats, and polished oak batten floor

14th November
As I put my hand on the bannister rail to go down the basement stairs, I thought of Charlie telling me of the time when he, standing in the same spot at the end of the hall, imitated Mrs Robinson's voice, calling downstairs, "George?" "Yes'm", came the reply followed by a chuckle from Charlie telling George he'd been had.
I am in a kind of reverie, with all that I have learned from Charlie & Pearl buzzing around my head. Now I know so much more about some of the characters who have lived here, I sometimes find myself half glancing over my shoulder perhaps to catch a glimpse of somebody going about their daily duties in another age.

December

3rd December
Moor Lane has been closed since Monday night. A vast expanse of water is our view across the moor.

4th December
The damn dog ran off again. He'd gone outside when Chris was closing up the chicken run at dusk. Last Saturday we had an 8am call to collect him from outside the Post Office. This evening the doctor found him skulking around behind the Health Centre.

7th December

How many ways can our chickens die? A few weeks ago a dog belonging to a friend of Lucy picked off one of our 4 Black Rocks. The friend dutifully bought a replacement & Lucy bought an extra pretty blue hen. Five hens. The pretty blue hen stepped under the wheel of a delivery van, & was squashed flat, cartoon style. It wasn't the driver's fault but he could have seemed a little sorry. Four hens. This morning, counting just 3 hens as they stepped down the ladder, I found the 4th dead in the hen house, perhaps from pining for its mate or frightened to death by the badger sniffing around last night. The kids have names for the badgers: Crazy Mike, Mad Pete, Alice & Tezza.

8th December

I awoke to dawn spreading across the sky & the sounds of early morning clear as a bell; cows lowing at Manor Farm, rooks & jackdaws swirling around our trees, dogs barking in the kennels at Newport. The wind must be coming from the south.

19th December
It's been a bright frosty, icy & sunny day. Lucy, Chris, James & the dogs bounded down onto the moor to skid on the ice. Betty says all the big houses hereabouts used to have a stock of skates for guests, the sort you'd fit on over your boots; she's seen them at the big house sales. Great expanses of frozen flooded moor were a more regular occurrence last century.

26th December
One o'clock, The Mummers Play in Queen Square, in their 19th year, with a very big crowd. It's an old traditional British folk play. I love it, even though the play is almost exactly the same each year. The pub was fit to bursting afterwards.

29th December

Heavy rain today, which will be with us until Thursday apparently. I drove down the muddy lanes to the farm to collect the goose for New Year's Day lunch, our custom these last 3 years, which gives a satisfying symmetry of bringing the year to a comforting full circle & a new beginning.

31st December

We still have 3 hens & a companionable little team they are. They come running to my call & are getting friendlier by the day, a wise move as it assures our vigilance towards their survival.

Afterword

Two men came to fit a new carpet in our sitting room recently. As the older of the two stepped through the front door, his gaze swept along the hall to the staircase. "I fitted the carpet on those stairs years ago", he said. He told me a very old lady had directed him in his work. "Mrs Stobart, Mrs Fox?" I asked, imagining an austere figure in sensible shoes.

His reply scooted me forward to the 1960s. "Oh no, she was in a tight leopard print dress". This must have been the sprightly Ruby Ward overseeing yet another change in the role of the house, this time from country club to private house once more.

Glimpses like these, a moment from years ago, sparkle in my mind's eye as I go about our house. The stories of lives lived here. In putting this book together there is a satisfaction, a relief, in having caught and netted reminiscences before they fade and disappear. I continue to keep half an eye on the past where there is plenty yet to be revealed, and the changing light and seasons draw my eye around to painting anew.

Acknowledgements

I would like to thank:

Mary Maher for her enthusiasm, encouragement and invaluable editing.

Betty Koppa and the North Curry Archives for welcoming me to access a wealth of knowledge and material, and for permission to publish a few items held at the Archives.

Charlie and Pearl Verrier for their hospitality and generosity in sharing their memories of this place.

Joanne Mears for her diligence and encouragement over an early draft.

Mike and Ken Hutchings for providing and verifying many anecdotes.

Kate Lynch for her practical help and advice.

Mary Stewart-Wilson for her encouragement, perceptive eye and details of her grandmother's time here.

Mary Rose Rogers, my aunt, who has shown a lively interest in this book from the start.

Katie Fforde for her ebullient interest in the project.

Raymond Briggs for his generous and helpful comments.

Somerset Heritage Centre for the use of the 1875 house plans (ref. D/D/bbm/213).

English Heritage for the use of the 1955 house particulars (ref. SA01629).

All my friends and neighbours who have contributed in so many ways to the setting down of this record.

Quantock Design Consultants for the design of the book.

And Simon, Eleanor, Lucy, Chris and James who are at the heart of the story.